KIDS: TECHNOLOGY AND THE FUTURE

Kids today are a new breed. The information technology revolution has transformed their lives and offers massive potential for their education and entertainment. Creativity, adaptability and emotional intelligence are the key skills they require. We need teachers who can nurture their voracious appetites for learning for this century. We need a responsive industry with innovative thinkers designing content, both for and with them.

Kids are seeking projects that inspire, but they are a tough audience to capture.

This essay describes examples from around the world of producers coming to grips with new technology and new ways of storytelling for children, building on their acute interest in learning from screen content. As the Australian Government is considering new television content regulations, this essay argues for a new approach to the development of wide-ranging innovative media projects for children's entertainment and education.

'Patricia Edgar has seen the landscape of children's media change over the past 50 years. In this essay she strikes a remarkable balance of appreciation for history and clear-eyed and optimistic views of the changing nature of digital media and children's use of those media today and in the future.

How smart this is: she argues for early and consistent media education, creative and innovative production of gaming, educationally purposeful and commercially successful media products for youth, and attention to media productions that offer a variety of diverse stories, characters and formats.

Moreover, she argues persuasively that youth need to be involved in these productions. She recognizes the importance of online safety and the role media play in preparing youth for citizenship and work-life.'

— Professor Ellen Wartella,
Al-Thani, Professor of Communication,
Director, Center on Media and Human
Development, Northwestern University, USA

'In this compact essay Patricia Edgar charts the ways forward for children's media. She does not belittle the challenges established broadcasters face from 'disruptive' new platforms, but she balances these with a plan for action focused on education and creativity. She calls for us all to teach children to 'read' the media, to discriminate truth from fiction and to be aware of the traps in both traditional and new media. She is all for children and young people having fun in their digital lives, but recognises they need leadership and creative solutions embracing the challeges of new and ever-evolving technologies. This is a must-read for anyone concerned with children's media.

I highly commend Patricia's invaluable contribution over the years, springing from her love for the world's next generations. And I share her concerns.'

— Dr Javad Mottaghi,
Secretary-General, Asia-Pacific
Broadcasting Union, Malaysia

KIDS: TECHNOLOGY AND THE FUTURE

Patricia Edgar

Australian Scholarly

Distributed by Australian Book Marketing,
a division of Australian Scholarly Publishing Pty Ltd
7 Lt Lothian St Nth, North Melbourne, Vic 3051
Tel: 03 9329 6963 / Fax: 03 9329 5452
enquiry@scholarly.info / www.scholarly.info

ISBN 978-1-925801-51-4

Cover design: Wayne Saunders

*To Frank Meaney, John Morris and Garth Boomer,
who helped me establish the Australian Children's Television
Foundation in 1982 , which kick-started an international
Australian children's production industry.*

*And to the members of the Board of the World Summit
on Media for Children Foundation, who have helped spread
the message around the world of the critical importance of
quality media for children: Adrian Mills, General Manager
BBC North; Anna Home, Chair of the Children's Media
Conference, UK; Per Lundgren, Senior Media Advisor for
the Nordic Council of Ministers; Professor Ellen Wartella,
Director, Center on Media and Human Development
at Northwestern University, USA; Dr Javad Mottaghi ,
Secretary General of the Asia-Pacific Broadcasting Union;
Patricia Castano, Founder Citurna Productions and
Imaginario, Colombia; and Chris Lovell, National Managing
Partner – Holding Redlich, Australia.*

*The first World Summit was held in Melbourne in
1996; since then Summits have been held on every continent.
A regional meeting will be held in Cartegena, Colombia,
March 2019, a Summit in Asia in 2020, and in Ireland in
2021 under the auspices of the World Summit on Media for
Children Foundation. www.wsmcf.com*

*And to Don Edgar for many things including the cartoon
overleaf.*

Can you get off that computer and watch TV?

Contents

The Future of
Children's Entertainment
and Education

Introduction:
The Need for Positive Media Literacy

The Information-technology Revolution is challenging the assumptions on which the education of children and the provision of their entertainment are based. The doomsayers and whistle-blowers from Silicon Valley are predicting anarchy and apocalypse. They argue, the big companies – Google, Facebook, Amazon, Apple, et al., AI, and the disrupters such as Uber and Air B&B – despite their rhetoric of preventing evil, promoting global togetherness and their potential to solve global issues, are in fact exacerbating inequality, poverty, unemployment, invasion of privacy, breakdown in social cohesion, political disruption and Donald Trump.[1]

On the other hand it is argued this revolution has the potential to transform lives for billions of people and solve the problems threatening the viability and sustainability of our planet. In this confused scenario how should we educate and entertain children to prepare them for the future?

Change often engenders fright and denial. The Reformation, the Renaissance, Galileo's scientific assertions that we were not the centre of the universe, the Industrial Revolution, the airplane, the atomic bomb were all game-changers prompting fierce debate. Every invention which has expanded communication, from the printing press onwards – comic books, movies, television, gaming and now social media – has led to claims such media are contributing to the decline of civilization and the destruction of childhood. So far, most of this hyperbolic critique has proven to be grossly over-stated. But unease is growing and the case against the technical behemoths mounting, as we move into the unpredictable world of AI and comprehending a seismic shift in the social order.[2]

In my view we need to be realistic; to be neither Cassandras nor Pollyannas; balance is a key concept for a successful transition into this technological era. Without technology human extinction could be inevitable, and it will be young people who must deal with the serious crises now facing the planet. We are on a path where the solutions to the big issues of the day – climate change, waste disposal, water-shortage, clean energy production, food supply, achieving social cohesion and economic sustainability on our planet, – can only be driven by technology. Most of us can't take to the bush and create a life off the grid. We must adapt as we transition to a different world. In this process we need visionary leadership and a first-class education for children which should begin at pre-school, with 3–6-year olds.

Small children, not capable of putting words together, can now access digital content on phones and tablets. By five or six kids can use social media to learn and stay in touch with parents and others. By seven to ten they are creating content by commenting on friends' posts and by eleven they are sharing personal photos, videos, stories and memes. Today the calls by paediatricians and concerned parents for children to spend no more than two hours per day across all electronic devices – laptops, smart phones, television, tablets, gaming devices and family computers to counter health problems, including brain damage, obesity, eye damage, postural problems, sleep deprivation, along with a host of psychological problems – are a pipe dream. Children's total daily media use (including multi-tasking with up to three devices at once) has been close to double figures for over a decade.[3] Today mobile phones have become an arm attachment for many youngsters who also sleep with them under their pillows. If we want to mediate the problems predicted from 'excessive' media usage, a creative solution, rather than a censorious approach, is what should be sought.

Because their media environment is not under the control of parents or teachers as it used to be, the distinctions between childhood and youth are blurring as maturity and 'knowing' come at an earlier age. Children today can access life in the wider world with the click of a finger, something not possible for previous generations. This has implications for their education and their media entertainment as they are often steps ahead of their teachers and parents, many of whom are unprepared to manage children's digital interests.[4] Twelve years ago I visited my grandson's primary school on grandparents' day. I sat with him and two friends as they told me they had hacked into the school's computer to access the internet. I was startled, reported what they told me, and their teachers, equally amazed, had to ask the boys how they had managed to do it.

While every media innovation has prompted child-activists to claim the minds and physical well-being of children are being damaged, their good intentions lose credibility through overreach. They often seem out of touch with the genuine interests and needs of the children they wish to protect. For example, my PhD research on the impact of violence in films and television on children did not support activists' dire predictions of violent behaviour influence. It showed children are much more discriminating, capable of reading images, genres and following the intent of a story than they are given credit for.[5]

Well-intentioned lobbyists, while very strong advocates for regulation, became one of the obstacles to the introduction of relevant contemporary Australian children's drama programming under the Australian Broadcasting Tribunal's (ABT) C classification in the late 1970's. Their idea of acceptable programming emphasized good role models in simple adventures which don't engage children for long and lead to bland programming. In 2008 Melinda Houston, the well-experienced television critic, wrote, 'Today's tween TV may be worthy but much of it is dull. It's the curse of the C classification. You know what they say about good intentions and the road to hell'.[6]

Part of the problem was, when the quota hour requirements were increased, series became longer, typically 26 episodes, and diversity in programming decreased. Generally speaking, the fewer episodes in a series the stronger the script ideas: think of the durable *Fawlty Towers* which was only twelve episodes in total, across two series.

The PC brigade continues its work today to police programs that 'rock the boat'. The latest example of their assiduity in wanting to protect teens is the response to the Netflix series *Insatiable,* a satirical take on bullying, fat-shaming, gender uncertainty and insatiable desires for food, booze and most things imaginable. Awareness of their bodies and 'poor body image' starts to develop as young as eight we are told.[7] *Insatiable* is an attempt to address the very issues it is being condemned for, which do pre-occupy teens. But one individual's petition to cancel the series gathered more than

118,000 signatures on Change.org in one day. Signatories decried the project as a 'tone-deaf' venture that encourages 'fat-shaming' on the basis of a two-minute promo alone.[8] Meanwhile others disagree and the show's lead Debby Ryan has 8.1 million followers on Instagram, 8 million on Facebook and four million on Twitter.[9]

Digital technology is creating resources of extraordinary potential but today's children see nothing new or remarkable in these devices. They have become an essential part of their world and mastery of their use has become a necessary life skill, as important as reading and writing, for living successfully in this century. So the more we understand these new technologies and the ways by which they can be deployed, the more effectively we will be able to use their power in the service of education, democracy, humanity and the future we build for younger generations. Given the complex global issues of our time, the need to educate young people about appropriate and innovative uses of digital media in all its forms is urgent.

There is to be a review of the use of smart phones in NSW schools led by the child psychologist Michael Carr-Greg, with some parents and schools calling for bans and limiting their use.[10] But before the panic takes hold we need to think this through. Children will continue to play, socialize and learn with their phones out of school, in their tertiary education and in the workplace. Students should be able to use their phones as tools for their learning, acquiring skills they will need for future careers. Phones can also be a lifeline to parents and crisis support, and medical apps can be important for some children in managing their health.[11] There are numerous positive reasons for their use, so why not a review into the potential of smart-phone use in schools in facilitating children's education, or, why not a review into new technology and its potential for education in the broadest sense?

Any review needs to start by accepting young people are no longer a passive audience to be dictated to about what they view and when they view it; they no longer wait for their favourite programs to be screened on scheduled television. Consequently while lobbyists, broadcasters and producers have resisted change, the viewing audience numbers for traditional television programs are tanking across the western world. Kids prefer to be gaming, producing their own ideas to put on YouTube, interacting on social media and self-learning, all of which they engage with enthusiastically. Educational institutions and children's entertainment media companies would strengthen the success of their mission by adapting to this new technology, making content relevant to the modern world, and working with their young students and viewers early.

Undoubtedly there are hazards for children in this online world and the lessons to be learned are complex. At an age when they are learning that Father Christmas, the Easter Bunny and the Tooth Fairy aren't real, we need to teach children that what they write or post on the internet will remain there forever. A cheeky, provocative 'selfie' or a bullying comment online, become part of a personal digital footprint able to be sourced by others, including future employers, indefinitely. A striking lesson in the way social media can bring someone down was the racist tweet from Roseanne Barr, the star of the sitcom *Rosanne*. It took twelve hours following her online description of a former advisor to President Obama as 'an ape', before her television series was cancelled, ending her career, despite her program's high ratings.[12] But responsible internet use can bring rewards and it is now a central part of our way of life.

Media literacy will be increasingly important, but we need a broader, more positive approach than has been taken so far. Children have to learn to interpret and navigate the 24/7 information overload so they can become informed participants in civil society. They need to understand that simply seeing cannot mean believing, that it is possible to construct reality; that what may seem to be improbable may indeed be true, and that what is thought to be fact may be 'fake news'. The President of the United States says, 'What you are seeing and hearing is not what is happening.' So who can be believed? We need a curriculum in schools that teaches understanding of factual news and information;

that persuasion is mixed in with entertainment and information to influence behaviour and attitudes, not only of consumers by advertisers, but by political propagandists to shape our beliefs. As Seymour Hersh, the investigative journalist who exposed the My Lai massacre in Vietnam has written, 'If your mother says she loves you, check it out!'[13]

The implications of AI, facial and voice recognition and issues related to invasion of privacy also require understanding, for many young people don't give a thought to sharing intimate personal details online. Big Brother is moving in on us and it is very confusing for the consumer to decide what to do about their personal data. Applicants for a visa to enter the US – an estimated 14.7 million people each year – will be asked, under proposed new State Department rules, to submit their social media user names for the past five years.[14] One prediction is that by 2020 China will be able to score each of their 1.4 billion citizens, based on their observed behaviour, down to how carefully they cross the street.[15] Where will such scrutiny lead? Education is the only practical and rational response.

Pre-school is not too soon to begin media literacy education as ideas and habits are shaped early. Recently I observed a child, of perhaps eighteen months, dummy in mouth, sitting in a high chair in a restaurant. She sat for two hours, without a peep, manipulating cartoon characters on an iPhone propped up in front of her while others talked and ate around her. Not long after, in a coastal diner, I watched a family – mum, dad and three children aged 3, 5 and 6 years of age – eating together: the kids each with a tablet and headphones. They were watching the movie *Frozen* as they ate their fish and chips. The little digital natives were engrossed in their technology. We underestimate children: their ingenuity, resilience, ability to learn and adapt, the creative ways by which they sort out their world and their social relationships, their drive for engagement and their enterprise.

Most of children's early brain development happens spontaneously, wherever they may be, as a result of playing with things and exploring their environment with innate curiosity and imagination. As they play, children learn the social strategies and skills they need to function as they are growing. Unfortunately instead of capturing and building on these natural attributes, schooling often crushes such spontaneity and produces conformity, by delaying knowledge acquisition through standardized curricula and resistance to new technology. As well, their entertainment media is too often stereotyped and banal.

Children learn in the home, the playground, at school and from the media which has now become a dominant force in their lives. Both media and education institutions have much to offer each other, particularly now, but the television industry, in particular, continues to eschew any whiff of education in their programs, believing the very mention of the word would deter the child audience. Equally, schools have resisted admitting media to the classroom, condemning commercial media's harmful influences, such as consumerism and banality; and they set up in competition. One pre-school teacher told me proudly the first thing she did at her school was put the computer in the cupboard. But children are now willingly and enthusiastically merging their education and entertainment, presenting an opportunity we would be remiss not to capitalize on.

The impact of computer games also needs to be viewed in a less negative way. Games, if purposely and creatively designed to meet each stage of child development, are a massive resource for teaching at pre-school and beyond. But many child advocates condemn most video games as anti-social and addictive; damaging to young minds through modeling graphic violent behaviour, sexual themes and profanity. What they have missed is the attraction games hold through social interaction and the analytical skills, dexterity, flexibility and adaptability required to play. There is a science to game-playing. No-one tells players what to do. They have to seek information and piece together data from many places to make sense of a game; they must make decisions quickly that have clear consequences. In doing so, they become experts at multi-tasking and parallel processing, learning to collaborate with others and compete in real time with players who can be from across the globe.

Recognizing that games could teach higher-order skills, and are especially attractive to the young natives growing up with digital technology, the Federation of American Scientists called on government, educators, and business to develop strategies to use video games to strengthen education and workforce training as far back as 2005. But few schools and educators responded to this call, leaving the commercial industry to take the initiative and reap the profits. It makes no sense to leave such a resource in the hands of commercial companies. Recent research by the Interactive Games and Entertainment Association (IGEA) shows that Australians alone spent more than $3 billion on video games in 2017.[16]

Before we make programs for them we must make the effort to set aside prejudice and understand our new child audience: we can no longer just serve them up what we, as adults, think is good for them. Aided by Silicon Valley, the study of audiences by the global entertainment industry has become a science. Evidence suggests that by merging age groups and cultures, the audience, which it feared would fragment into minority groups and no longer achieve 'mass' scale, has in fact expanded. This is seen in gaming, superhero brand franchise movies and even the burgeoning graphic book industry where the revival of comics, with all their diversity, has become main-stream with serious art and sophisticated stories. In 2018 the list for the Man Booker Prize included a graphic novel in recognition that one of the oldest forms of storytelling in the world, the comic, is a literary form. Some of the most original graphic work in the world is being created in Australia.[17]

Technology offers the entertainment industry economic benefits and offers the education sector greater appeal and effectiveness for teaching and learning. Given the speed of change in communication technology and the ways by which children are using and inhabiting media, it is time to encourage collaboration between the media and schools for the future of children and a 21st century education. The most important question is how might this best be done?

The Changing World of Children's Media Entertainment

Teachers and education policy-makers need to understand better than they have how powerful a force media are in children's lives and should work towards harnessing their potential. As the audience takes more control, the media industry's response to the information technology revolution demonstrates an ability to adapt and experiment in some sectors but turmoil in others.

Print media and broadcasting have been slow to respond to new technology, fruitlessly trying to put up barricades and retain their protected privileges, with print the biggest loser. We have watched the incredible shrinking Fairfax Press (now subject to a takeover by Nine Entertainment Co or NEC), and we hear the persistent calls by News Limited for the ABC to remain off-line; a demand that would see the national broadcaster out of business and the diversity of our news and current affairs coverage seriously diminished.

The commercial broadcasting industry is demanding increased government protection by reduced license fees, cutbacks to the ABC and abolition of the thirty-eight-year-old Australian quota requirements, while the independent production industry lobbies to retain quotas claiming, rhetorically, they are, 'creating Australian dreams'. That ideal disappeared a long time ago as the broadcasting media and the producers worked out how to game the system.[18] Limited creative and innovative thinking is now being applied to children's media to meet the needs and interests of the 21st century audience. As the Government is currently reviewing Australian and Children's screen content the question is, what kind of media programs for children justify support by Government regulation and taxpayer subsidy?

Children's television quotas were designed when traditional broadcasters were dominant in the late seventies. There was no children's production industry in Australia at that time and programs screened came from the UK and the USA. Our children did not see Australian locations, hear Australian voices or see themselves on screen. We had an insidiously demeaning cultural environment where the cringe was rife and Australians grew up believing we had no place of importance in the world. All that mattered took place in the 'old country' or the USA. As a film fan that was where I wanted to go. I didn't realize that I craved *Australian* stories, but making them would become my mission. I got my chance when I was appointed to chair the first Inquiry into Program Standards, for the Australian Broadcasting Control Board (ABCB) in 1976. That Advisory Committee recommended a plan for programming for children under 13 years that later became the Children's Television Standards (CTS or C classified programs) implemented by the Australian Broadcasting Tribunal (ABT) in 1979.[19] They are still in force. Their introduction incensed the television networks which argued there was no such thing as a children's program, our kids couldn't act and they wouldn't watch any program made locally. They were proven wrong.

The Australian children's drama quota, designed to respond to the call for local stories, was introduced in 1984 and never intended as an industry assistance scheme. Developing successful children's drama was a challenge. There was much advice about what was not acceptable but very little about what children really wanted to watch. In the end programming that the audience welcomed did not emerge through rules exhorting what must *not* be done – no violence, no stereotyping, no depiction of bullying, nudity, or swearing – or asserting characters must present positive role models. Such rules are no guide to storytelling. Shows that children want to watch come from an understanding of audience interests and not from politically correct rules. The breakthrough in programming for children and young people came when creative producers took risks, thought outside conventional genres and left behind didacticism, simple-minded adventures, and political correctness.

If, as a producer, you are true to your culture, and get things right, children everywhere will respond to a well-told story. *Round the Twist* was the exemplar. With the brilliant team of Esben Storm as Director and Paul Jennings as co-writer we succeeded beyond our wildest dreams. *Round the Twist* became a cult series and a model children's program. It challenged the mores of children's television, demonstrating young people had their own culture and sense of fun.

The program, which had genuine Aussie spirit and humour, was spoken in the Australian idiom, and no PC compromises were made. Around the world children related to the series and, as it happened, adults who remembered their childhood did as well. The very things that kids thought riotously funny were what made the PC brigade uncomfortable. When the Minister for Communications visited location during production, he was startled to see Pete Twist ready to go on set looking all of nine months pregnant. Pete had peed on a tree sprite and that was the result. 'What do people say about this sort of thing?' The Minister asked me. 'They laugh', I replied. The BBC's imprimatur helped the program gain acceptance with other cautious broadcasters and the production, as well as promoting Australia and the Great Ocean Road, encouraged kids to read. *Round the Twist* helped reshape the way producers viewed the child audience and became the first television program financed by the Australian Film Finance Corporation – for adults or children – to go into profit. It still attracts the child audience and it is now forgotten what a breakthrough the program was. It is an example of the kind of thinking Australian children's media production needs now, experimentation and innovation.

While traditional television ratings have slumped, the Silicon Valley entrepreneurs have vigorously gone after their audience, making Facebook a $500+ billion company with 2.2 billion active monthly users uploading more than 8 billion digital images a day.[20] YouTube, the most popular viewing site with young people, is unbeatable competition for conventional television. Every day it has 5 billion views and it offers a place where children can find content that reflects their interests as well as upload their own expressions and seek a following. Netflix comes in next with more young viewers than view traditional broadcasting. The iconic broadcaster, the BBC, once a dominant world player in children's television, has found more than 80% of their potential audience goes to YouTube for on-demand content, half go to Netflix and fewer than 20% now go to the BBC. Children in the UK, aged five to fifteen, spend more time each week online (15 hours and 18 minutes on average) than they do watching television. The average weekly reach of CBBC, the BBC's Channel for 6- to 12-year olds, has fallen dramatically and the growth of CBBC online has not compensated for the fall. As well, 43% of the age group uses their mobile phones to watch television.[21]

The BBC has been struggling to stall their audience exit, making their biggest investment in children's content and services in a generation. One response to child-centric social apps like Facebook Messenger and LEGO Life, is CBBC Buzz, a new mobile community for under 13's. Forty fresh pieces of content – ultra-short videos, GIF's, challenges, quizzes and memes – are dropped in before and after school each day. Users can generate content but the drop-in material is based around its branded programs.[22] Still the BBC child audience continues its fall. Money is not the problem; it is ideas.

Ofcom, the UK regulator, is reviewing children's content on television and online and published a review update in July 2018 which asks British Public Service Broadcasters to 'develop and share their plans to address their concerns' about the lack of diverse quality programming for children. The report concedes children's viewing habits have fundamentally changed and they are watching a wide variety of content across a range of platforms. It argues that setting quotas would not be an effective approach; that reaching children means exploiting the opportunities presented by the internet; that broadcasters should explore new and innovative ways of providing them with what they need and want; and that a range of genres can contribute to this representation of children's lives.[23] Ofcom correctly lists the problems but is looking to the broadcasters to define a solution. In my view they ignore the most important issue that could help solve this dilemma: the role of education in the program mix.

The BBC is not alone in losing audience; the fundamental change in children's viewing behaviour is global. Nickelodeon, Viacom's global children's channel, has suffered the same fate with ratings for children aged between 2 and 11 down 25% in a year. Experienced producers are being shown the door as the Channel searches for a solution.[24] In Australia, independent producers are lobbying the Government to legislate for quotas on every media platform including the ABC. They hold up the UK as a model reason why subsidized, regulated, quotas should be retained, cherry-picking the data and neglecting to mention the problems being faced there.[25] Ofcom specifically states in its interim report that quotas are not an effective answer. Meanwhile the ABC is no longer insisting its digital children's channels are a great success. Across the globe this migration of children from traditional broadcasting will only increase as Apple and Amazon roll out their programs. In the digital media world, creativity, innovation and risk-taking by producers will be the only way forward.

There is no question it is a major challenge for the traditional media businesses to find a viable economic model in the face of the advancing behemoths – hence the move to mergers and takeovers. Nine and Fairfax are simply the first in Australia, where the disruption of the advertiser-based model of the television and entertainment industries is requiring new relationships and rescheduling of content according to audience interests. In this environment a vibrant children's media industry will only be achieved if established thinking is shaken to its core.

Re-thinking TV

It is not surprising that the Norwegian public television network NRK is leading by example. They have always been innovators in children's television. In September 2015, NRK released a teen drama called SKAM into a fragmented, multi-platform, on-demand, time-shifting environment. These are the very characteristics that, the Australian independent producers argue, put our traditional children's drama at risk.[26] There is nothing remarkable about the overall narrative of SKAM. Essentially the program is about what it feels like to be a teenager at high school and the heartbreaks, rivalries, friendships and rejections involved in this difficult life stage. But this series is an experiment with modern media formats.

The Norwegian creator of SKAM, Julie Andem, began where producers need to begin, by talking with her audience about what they were watching and the ways they were using social media. She then devised a format that capitalized on the way kids jump from screen to screen. The project began with a six-minute clip appearing on Facebook Watch, the social network's entertainment portal, with no advertising or pre-publicity. It aroused curiosity and word of mouth led the PR campaign. The characters had social media accounts with photos, video-clips and comments to give them depth. There were many hidden layers which made SKAM like a multi-layered detective show where all the seemingly disparate activities and digital platforms formed into a single narrative which took initiative to unravel. The production was able to respond to fan feedback and change plot details, with the result that the fictional social media of SKAM generated real social media. The series ran for four seasons. France, Germany, Italy and the US, have now produced their own versions.

SKAM is a seminal, creative response to the multi-platform world the kids inhabit that worked. The approach would defy the understanding of many adults and producers it seems. So what's the value? The program has its roots in public television and has an educational and social purpose. In an article for the *New Yorker Magazine*,[27] titled 'Posts Modern', Andem, the originator, defined the series' aim as 'to educate its young audience and raise self-esteem, helping them become capable of being individuals who can make decisions on their own'. A theme of the program is, 'If you keep trying things will come out in the end', an important lesson for teens to learn.

The challenge in Australia now is for the government and the Australian Communications and Media Authority (ACMA) to identify a new regulatory structure to encourage innovation in programming to capture the benefits of this new technology in the interests of children while keeping them safe online. We need to be telling Australian stories still, but in diverse formats and to a global audience – this is the big change.

Gaming resources

Live-action drama is not the only important format. Games provide well-established learning opportunities and are equally important, as is the support of children's own productions and original ideas that encourage their collaboration online. Kids have voted with their feet; pre-schoolers are the only kids left whose viewing can be controlled, but then only up to a point, for parents are seeing their toddler can walk up to a screen, swipe it, and express frustration when it does not respond.

Alongside innovation in series formats, we need to see experiments with narrative gaming. Educational opportunities here are unlimited. A recent phenomenon, *Fortnite,* has led to an expansion of the game-playing target audience capturing children, young people and gamers generally (reports have varied between 40–120 million globally: a lot anyway). And it has done so by changing many of the expectations of video games. While parents still worry about the time kids want to play this game, it is a kid-friendly, safe environment, and although a third-person-shooter game, its violence is cartoon-like. There is no blood, gore or threatening menace. No knives. According to the Wall Street Journal many parents are playing with their kids, even paying for coaching.[28] It can be played by up to one hundred gamers including teams of friends who support one another and is clearly a lot of fun. Its lack of misogyny, racism, and its appeal to inexperienced gamers, who can learn together, no doubt contributes to the fact that girls are playing in large numbers, something the game industry has been trying to achieve for two decades. The challenge for parents and teachers should be to recognize the game can teach children how to apply strategies, and how to socialize while they encourage balance.

Adaptation and innovation needed

Adaptation must be the name of the game in children's entertainment generally. The movie industry, like the gaming industry, studies its audience and responds by accommodating special groups. Young people are the primary target at the multiplexes where superheroes have dominated the box office over the last decade, but in 2017 the two blockbusters that broke the mold were *Wonder Woman* and *Black Panther*. Women are in. As a result Marvel's first 'superheroine' character the Wasp, who was created in a comic book 55 years ago, has a starring role in *Ant Man and the Wasp* and Scarlett Johansson will star as the *Black Widow* in her own movie. *Captain Marvel* will make her debut as a female superhero played by Brie Larson in 2019. The interesting thing about the character of Captain Marvel, Carol Danvers, is she grew up with an abusive father, was not allowed to attend university, and after joining the Avengers was abducted and raped by a supervillain, named Marcus Immortus. Danvers symbolizes the troubled history of women in mainstream comics. But in the latest film version she is no token female. 'There may never have been a superhero so intrinsically linked to the survival of humanity as Captain Marvel, whom the studio has pitched as Earth's best hope in the fight against Thanos (a figure even the Hulk found himself cowering before).'[29]

Marvel has gone from having no women as heroes in their comic stable to having twenty. Margaret Stohl, who is writing the Danvers story says, 'It's a great time to be a female creator … Kids are seeing themselves as Wonder Woman, they'll see themselves as Captain Marvel … young people are listening, they want it. This is for them'.[30] She's right.

Matt Groening, the creator of *The Simpsons*, using his own family as his reference, showed us successfully what family life was really like. He is trying something different, turning his attention to the fantasy genre with a new animated series called *Disenchantment* sending up the genre. His lead is Princess Bean who has a mind of her own and is always in trouble. Groening says female characters in fairy-tale classics, 'whether kindhearted or wicked they take risks, they talk back and they eventually get what they want'.[31] Groening believes his new heroine will strike a chord with young viewers.

Lesbians, gays and bi-sexuals are all starring as superheroes as producers and distributors recognize that social diversity does not necessarily mean fragmentation and shrinking audience numbers, when there is a global audience to exploit on multiple platforms. Even Disney is getting in on the diversity bandwagon, casting Jack Whitehall as a lead gay man in the feature film *Jungle Cruise*. Only the fact he is straight is causing controversy.[32] Australian actor Ruby Rose will play the first openly gay superhero in a TV series with her latest role as Batwoman. The character first appeared in the DC Comics universe as a romantic interest for Batman to dispel suggestions of his homosexuality, mainly in response to Senate subcommittee hearings in 1954 investigating the impact of comic books on juvenile delinquency. Batwoman has been openly gay in the comic books since 2006 when she was reintroduced as a lesbian of Jewish descent who found a love interest in former Gotham police detective Renee Montoya. DC Comics representatives said at the time that they made the decision to better reflect social diversity.

'This is a childhood dream,' said Ruby Rose. 'This is something I would have died to have seen on TV when I was a young member of the LGBT community who never felt represented on TV and felt alone and different,' she wrote.[33]

Superheroes are also gaining weight as the audience members expand their waistlines. Mr. Incredible is a plus size and Faith Herbert, the telekinetic superhero in Valiant's comic universe, created in 1992, but now to star in a live action movie, has a double chin and a skin-tight jumpsuit, keeping her sizeable curves in order.

And there is a new genre of 'desk-top movies' – that is narratives that take place entirely within a computer screen – attracting young audiences. They include: *Noah*, a seventeen-minute film which screened at the Toronto International Film Festival, about relationships online, which illustrates the flitting attention span and lack of true connection in digital culture; *Unfriended,* an ingenious supernatural horror film where several high school friends find themselves terrorized online by an anonymous person; and *Searching*, a main-stream Hollywood thriller, shot from the point-of-view of smart-phones and computer screens, which follows a father trying to find his missing 16-year-old daughter. Both *Unfriended* and *Searching* are financed by a Russian director-producer, Timur Bekmambetov, who has ambitious plans to make 50 such films each year. He is motivated by the fact that *Unfriended*, his first attempt, received mixed reviews from critics, but was a massive box office success, grossing $64 million against a $1 million budget. The desktop genre is a cheap, profitable and relatively quick way to make movies.[34] However Bekmambetov will need some immensely talented writers to come up with engaging stories to meet his plan. Meanwhile, a pink *Pepper Pig* has captured the toddlers.[35]

The regulatory response must also change

In such a dynamic media environment broadcasting regulation is an exceptionally tricky exercise. If they are to work, regulations require creative application and on-going monitoring as commercial players will always seek to out-maneuver them. Bureaucracies move slowly. It takes time to define, then to pass legislation and once regulations are in place, too often assumptions are made that the job is done. That is almost never the case.

When the Children's Television Standards (CTS)

were first enacted a diversity of programming resulted for a few years, during which time an international Australian quality children's production industry was established. The Australian system of regulation of children's programs was seen as a model for other countries and the envy of many children's producers around the world. It took just a few years before the networks and the producers found ways to exploit the system. They complied with the law, with the least possible expenditure of funds, but certain independent producers made hay. Cheap, unimaginative animation, created for the international market, became accepted as equivalent to original Australian drama. Long-running series, that could have been made anywhere, were devised by Australian producers who ran successful businesses in partnership with overseas broadcasters, supplying them with a regular source of programs generously subsidized by the Australian tax-payer. In some cases Australian 'producers' fronted programs that were scripted and creatively controlled overseas but were using Australian funding.

The C system was officially shown to be dying in 1999 when the Australian Broadcasting Authority (ABA) published its report on '20 years of C',[36] which commented on the low production values resulting from the trend to longer series that reduced the variety of children's programs produced and broadcast. Since then children's programming has continued to lose its audience and is, generally, formulaic and uninspiring. There has scarcely been a program of note on commercial television as a result of quotas since that report. The few worthwhile programs that have emerged have come from the ABC, doing the job it should be doing, and they have been outside the quota requirements. Yet Australian lobbyists and producers, in response to the current review, continue to ask for more of the same: to retain the forty-year-old quotas and expand them across all platforms.

A Drama Quota for children – that is stories produced by adults to be programmed during defined timeslots – is no longer practical and no longer represents the media most children enjoy and need. Stories and other experiences, which provide lessons for life, are vital for children's development, but they can now be accessed online in many guises. Children's self-exploration through social media is one form; their own simple productions and collaborating on projects with friends are others. Kids can be gripped equally by a good story on a podcast as on a television screen. They can listen on the move. They can click through what's on offer: a cornucopia from which they are learning and having fun. A flimsy plot won't hold them.

A new plan for children's programming should be born from an enlightened and positive approach and a clear understanding of the needs and interests of the child audience it is intended to serve in 2019. Children should participate in this process. Programs must be multi-platform and innovative in concept. A producer should first ask, 'Do I have something to say and offer to children that goes beyond the business of feeding the beast and drawing a subsidy?' A producer with the interests of children at heart thinks about ideas not brands, characters not merchandise, originality and challenge not recycled plots and clichés. It is the producers' job to attract children, otherwise they have no right to subsidy and regulatory support.

In the transformed media landscape, where young people have moved to the platforms built by new mammoth global players, we need to ask what they are doing there and work with the ingredients that attract them. We have a lot to learn about this audience. For the first time since television was introduced in 1956 children's interests merge media with education. As well, the audience that broadcast television has found these most difficult to reach, teenagers, are using multi-platform media enthusiastically. YouTube, gaming and social media attract teens and Netflix is clearly going after them with shows like *Stranger Things, To the Bone, Insatiable, 13 Reasons Why*,[37] and producing 'rom-coms' with young leads. In Australia it's time we went after the child and youth audience with the best projects our creative practitioners can offer.

How Can Education Merge with Entertainment for the Benefit of Children?

For most of my fifty-year career in education, communication research, policy development and production I have been working toward a closer integration of media production and education for children. As far back as 1977 I argued, 'Television is having a much greater influence than schools on a large number of Australian children. The universities need to carry out the research necessary to identify the problems associated with television and then assist in the production of programs that offer enrichment and life experiences that go some way to filling the gaps in people's lives when they turn to television as their major companion.'[38]

My partner in lobbying and a member of the Advisory Committee on Program Standards in 1976 and my Deputy Chair of the ABT's Children's Program Committee (CPC) was Frank Meaney, an inspector of schools in the NSW Education System. Later we worked together establishing the Australian Children's Television Foundation (ACTF). We assisted the Hon. Norman Lacey and the Hon. Paul Landa, the Education Ministers in Victoria and NSW respectively, to take to the Australian Education Council of Ministers (AEC), the idea that an ACTF be established to produce exemplary programming for children. Ministers for the Arts and Education from around Australia endorsed the concept. I was appointed founding Director and Frank Meaney was appointed to my Board. From the outset every program produced by the ACTF was based on a sound educational concept. In time this approach proved to be the programs' strength and the basis of their durability. The first anthology series *Winners* was accompanied by books written by the scriptwriters from their original screenplays and accompanied by teaching materials. The eight novels, published with the release of the programs, remained in print for more than ten years and set a pattern for publishing with children's programs.

The ACTF's most ambitious project *Lift Off* (1990), an early childhood program with financial backing from the Robert Holmes à Court Foundation, was a comprehensive education package with a television series, music and video tapes, books, a magazine, games, curriculum materials and an out-reach program in every State. Garth Boomer, an eminent educator of the time, persuaded all State Directors of Curriculum to endorse *Lift Off* and produce curriculum materials to support the series. It was a first in Australia. This project was set to challenge *Sesame Street* globally, as its educational basis was broader and incorporated Harvard educational psychologist Professor Howard Gardner's ground-breaking multiple intelligences theory, as a basis for its content.[39] *Sesame Street* was by then more than 20 years old. The Children's Television Workshop's marketing manager came to Melbourne to offer a deal to buy *Lift Off* outright and put it on the shelf so it could not compete with *Sesame Street* which itself had been a serious attempt to integrate an entertainment program with educational goals, developed in the late 1960s.

They needn't have worried as the ABC, in one of its most self-serving decisions, took the program off air so it could not compete with their in-house productions, notably *Bananas in Pyjamas* and *Play School*. That is a story told elsewhere.[40] Paddy Conroy, the Head of Television at the ABC, a strong advocate for *Lift Off* had fallen on his sword, along with Nick Collis-George, Head of Children's programs, over the back-door sponsorship of entertainment programs on the ABC. A producer who had worked on *Bananas in Pyjamas* took over, and *Lift Off,* an $18 million resource, widely acknowledged by educators around Australia and globally as a break-through education/media project, was shelved; children were the losers. There has been nothing of that dimension, with that philosophy and ambition produced since.

I continued to design ACTF programs with an education core until I stepped down as Director in 2002. Then the direction changed. The ACTF became a distributor for independent producers. Independents do not have the resources or the incentive to invest in long-term development of an idea, which is what quality programming requires, and children's programs attract lower pre-sales than adult programming. The *raison d'être* for the ACTF when it was established was to innovate and be true to the child audience, taking the risks in production a commercial producer can't afford to take.

That said, history and technology have now exposed the inertia of Australian producers generally. Much more than broadcast television quotas is now required to serve the needs and interests of today's children. Their fundamentally changed media usage calls for a radical shift in the thinking behind the production of programs for them and in the media literacy curriculum they are taught from pre-school to Year 12. If these policies could be combined it would be the most effective response to capturing the potential of multi-platform diverse children's programming, their social media and new technology use, and dealing with the problems social media are exposing. The comprehensive aim of such programs and curricula should be to prepare children for a new world, strengthening a desirable civil culture, through supporting schools, tertiary institutions, children's media entertainment and their transition from school to the workplace.

A fast-encroaching new media information order is unstoppable and 'coddling' a generation will only exacerbate problems.[41] We need to be clear that used responsibly, social media has many beneficial effects for the social development of children and adolescents, enhancing their education, well-being and cohesion by connecting them to peers with similar interests at home and across the globe.

The naysayers must be kept in perspective. We know that social media can be successful in promoting conspiracy theories, racism, misogyny and hatred. Bullying, always a problem with children and teenagers, has become an epidemic on social media; revenge imaging is apparently rife, as is the transmission of abusive images, but the best way to counter cruel and negative behaviour is by education. Parents need to play their part and know how their young children engage with social media but the education system must assist them, providing lessons on appropriate use of technology.[42] Some activists are demanding Facebook and Apple lift their game, with investors calling for these companies to develop new software tools that would help parents control and limit their children's smart-phone use: a reasonable demand.[43] Aligning with them are powerful tech avengers with inside Silicon Valley experience who have joined forces in the US and are finding sympathetic ears with their calls for regulation.[44] But what happens next?

In the process we must not lose sight of the potential of these mammoth media companies. Governments do need to insist they meet their obligations, financially and ethically and accept responsibility for their adverse influences on social behaviour and the algorithms that undermine democratic processes. Regulations, however difficult to define, are required to police their uncivil behaviour, but they must be practical, adaptable and supported by an education campaign. They should include a focus on developing media as a positive resource for children.

What Are the Issues That Need to Be Addressed in This Social, Economic and Political Transition?

1. Ensuring safety online

The first lesson for children to learn about the internet is a precautionary one for they are instinctively attracted to what it has to offer them. It has always been the case that when children venture alone into the outside world for the first time they must learn survival skills – they must look both ways before crossing the road and be wary of strangers. Now there is another imperative – they must know how to behave online.

In teaching cyber-safety and the rules of online social engagement, kids need to understand the difference between what can be displayed publicly and what should remain private; how to block people who harass them and to avoid clicking randomly. They need to understand the code implicit in receiving and sending personal messages, the hazards of instant feedback, the ways to record, create, compose and communicate with peers in and beyond the classroom. These intelligent tools they can now access, not only allow communication and collaboration with friends socially and formally, they facilitate inquiry, note keeping, referencing, learning and documentation, all of which add up to a digital footprint. Now employers can google job-applicants to check their suitability, having no footprint can be as disadvantageous as having a poorly-managed one. So children need to learn early how to curate a positive footprint which will become an asset for them in the future. They can share their achievements and interests: school projects, awards, pieces of writing, and digital artworks; they can expand their social contacts and self-learning, but anti-social commentary and provocative 'selfies' should be taboo online.

The smart schools are designing programs to teach their students the skills they need to help manage their devices and their use: break up prolonged periods of engagement; turn off devices before bedtime; keep them physically away from the head; use text of easily readable size; understand password security; block people who harass them and don't click on anything questionable. While communicating with friends is the most popular online activity, and the one that gets some parents upset, children will use the internet for a variety of purposes, including homework, gaming, watching videos and seeking new information. New media have opened up a wider world than ever before experienced. While facilitating their access to information, they have given children a voice and a means of distribution. These are all tools that could assist them to build a new world fit for their future, if managed well. They are central to the process of breaking down educational, social and cultural barriers, reducing conflict and building tolerance across the globe. Strengthening these attributes is our challenge.

2. Merging educational purpose and commercial benefit

It makes no sense for us to leave the development of media products for children in the hands of the commercial entertainment industry while kids are forced to 'power down' when they enter the classroom. If this inertia continues, the disconnection between children's everyday lives and their experience of formal education will grow from a gap to a chasm and schools as we know them, like traditional media institutions, will become redundant.

A good teacher is invaluable, but too many teachers lack the technological know-how to be effective in the modern classroom, for they try to adapt technology to reinforce old ways of thinking. Even if such teachers could be retrained there will never be enough of them to go around. So we have to find ways to use them more effectively, as well as explore new ways of learning. Progress in teaching literacy skills is of fundamental importance for children across the globe, for in 2015 the UN reported that up to 100 million children are not in school. Media can assist in reaching these children and helping their development.

Games have moved from the arcade to the pocket and offer significant business opportunities for those who know what they are doing. And there is no area of education to which they cannot be applied. The first real game companies started in Finland in the late 1990s and there are now around 250 companies operating there, employing around 3,000 people and generating about 0.5% of the country's GDP. With mobile they see the market as of infinite size and in that space a game can be tweaked until it's right, making it easier to succeed with a project, both with the intended audience and financially.

Finland is consistently ranked as having one of the most effective educational systems in the world. Its teachers are highly qualified academically and so it is not surprising that they are utilizing new technology effectively. Finland's gaming sector is very successful and working with the education sector in the interest of children while creating profitable business models. The two creatives, Peter Vesterbacks and Lauri

Konttori, who brought *Angry Birds* to the world (which at its height had 3 billion downloads) are now leading a company that wants to bring education and gaming together. They have raised more than $9 million to start up a Helsinki-based company called Lightneer. Its first game – a joint venture with the Universities of Harvard, Oxford, Helsinki and Cern – is to make subjects such as physics palatable, to even the youngest children. 'Pok'emon for particles' is how they describe *Big Bang Legends* in which each of the 118 atoms of the periodic table is given its own personality and can be collected by players. It is an entertaining way to learn all the elements. Lightneer is targeting chemistry, biology, languages, geography, 'whatever' to make education more effective. The global education market is estimated by the *Angry Birds'* entrepreneurs to be worth about 6.3 trillion euros and they are aiming at capturing ten per cent of that market.[45]

There are other interesting examples of innovative educational games overseas. At *Quest to Learn,*[46] in New York, games are at the core of the curriculum. Quest believes games motivate students to collaborate and learn by doing. They define games as carefully designed, student-driven systems that are narrative-based, structured, interactive and immersive. Games, they say, let students know if they are failing or succeeding at a moment's notice and allow them to retry, or 'iterate,' after a failure or loss. Unlike traditional educational systems, failure is a necessary and integral part of the 'game.' It creates a context for students to be motivated to try again and succeed. Learning experiences in games don't feel like spoon-fed education, they feel like play.

Game-based learning takes a variety of forms at *Quest to Learn*. For instance, in ninth grade biology, students spend the year as workers in a fictional bio-tech company, and their job is to clone dinosaurs and create stable ecosystems for them. By inhabiting the role of biotech scientists, the students learn about genetics, biology and ecology. Sixth graders use *Adventures with Dr. Smallz,* a microscopic, absent-minded doctor lost in a patient's body who sends the class communiques to help him diagnose and cure. Students play the role of designers, scientists, doctors and detectives as they explore cellular biology and the human body. In *Galactic Mappers*, a social studies game about physical geography, students compete in teams to create the most geographically diverse continent in a shared hemisphere. This group-mapping project encourages students to collaborate, design, iterate, and present a finished product in a single class period. And ninth graders use *Storyweavers,* a collaborative storytelling role-playing game.

These games not only engage students in the learning process, but also allow teachers to assess students in real time and provide feedback on learning experiences immediately.

3. Developing civic skills to participate in a democratic community

Perhaps no area of programming for children is more important today than educating them to acquire skills to participate and take action effectively in our increasingly complex world. This is a critical time in our history. It is claimed the basic tenets of democracy are being eroded as there is disenchantment with political and corporate institutions. Global media forces, the like of which have never been known, are manipulating and influencing behaviour and affecting issues that will determine the future viability of the planet and its burgeoning population. News values are in dispute. The mission expressed by Google and Facebook to create a fully connected planet sharing common ideals seems to have misfired.[47] Given the confusion imposed by fake news what should we be doing to best help children and youth play a meaningful role in democratic institutions and face up to the issues of inequality, climate change and sustainability, in a global polarized political climate? Such questions are occupying researchers who are working with the Macarthur Research Network on Youth and Participatory Politics (YPP) in the USA on the Good Project based at Harvard University with support from Professor Howard Gardner. They have assembled The Digital Civics Toolkit, designed to help youth explore, recognize, and take seriously the civic potentials of digital life. The toolkit contains five modules, each capturing a key practice associated with digital civics: participation, investigation, dialogue, voice and action.

'The serious study of media should be recognized as a legitimate study in schools and universities today. Students need to understand how all forms of media function, how they are controlled and how they disseminate information and promote an ideology. Without this knowledge it is impossible for individuals to make a critical evaluation of events in society. The media are dominant political, social and cultural forces and as such should be analysed by political scientists, sociologists, psychologists, historians, lawyers, critics, aestheticians and philosophers.'[48]

These words, written in 1977, are even more pertinent today as we are inundated with political content across all available platforms – social media, TV, streaming services, YouTube, podcasts and internet message boards. The Ofcom Content Review draws attention to 'the limited range of children's programs that help children of all ages understand the world around them.'[49]

In the UK, the BBC, which has been hit by a youth exit from their news services, is launching a national training program in schools to help young people 'identify real news and filter out fake or false information'.[50] There is no shortage of content relevant to such training. President Trump's theatrical promotion by Destiny Pictures screened to North

Korean leader Kim Jong-un at their Singapore Summit is one example of propaganda worthy of study.

One of the ABC's achievements for children is the program *Behind the News* (*BtN*) which has been on air for 48 years (barring 2004 when it was axed through funding cuts). It is aimed at upper primary and lower secondary students to help them understand the major news stories of the week, providing background information not usually given in news bulletins. A similar program *ttn* (*the total news*), debuted on Network Ten, in the year *BtN* was not on air but was axed in 2008.

Young people can now express their concern about issues that affect them directly and they are doing so with variable consequences.[51] In the wake of the massacre at the High School in Parkland Florida, young Americans carried the gun control message across the nation so successfully, young people across the world joined in. This protest will be ongoing as 'nineteen kids are shot every day in the United States'.[52] At Melbourne's Trinity Grammar School in 2017 a high-profile social media campaign led to the reinstatement of a popular teacher who had been sacked for cutting a boy's hair. In Dhaka, Bangladesh, in August 2018, thousands of students paralyzed parts of the capital to protest the country's abysmal road safety conditions. Teenagers dressed in school uniforms erected checkpoints across the city, forcing the police and government ministers to observe traffic laws that are otherwise poorly enforced. The police reacted with violent force.

This is a world where the self-described 'most powerful man in the world' communicates by Twitter. This gives him his own voice, immediate, unfiltered, unchallenged and unexamined. He has a wider reach than the celebrated press of the *New York Times* or the *Washington Post* so we are in uncharted territory and education about this world has to be a top priority.

One of the best ways for children to learn to understand media and its capacity to excite, to capture, to influence or to manipulate truth is by making films themselves. The ABC program *My Year 7 Life* explores the experiences young people are having during this critical transition year. Sixteen students document their lives, preoccupations, fears and achievements over 18 episodes, speaking direct to camera. This collaboration between the producers and the media-savvy target audience teaches them how to use their own voices effectively. The result is a compelling factual program.

Films made by young people do not need to be expensive; they can be made simply with digital equipment including smart phones. The means of their distribution to friends and a global audience is a click of a finger; word of mouth does the rest. The scripting, photographing, acting, editing and sound mixing of a narrative, documentary or fiction, add layers to a construction of 'reality' through image-making. Support for this activity for children is as worthy of subsidy as any adult-produced drama or animation made for them.

There are global initiatives springing up to encourage and showcase kid's productions with partnerships between Foundations, media producers and educators around the world. In Greece, 'Fest of Fests' held its inaugural meeting in July 2018. Supported by the Michael Cacoyannis Foundation, based in Athens, this venture is establishing an online community emphasizing the development of critical and informed viewers and supporting filmmaking by youngsters around the world. They will run an annual forum showcasing initiatives and exchanging innovative ideas to support film and digital literacy.

Around the world there are many well-regarded programs applying new media to transform education going well beyond civic skills. Some examples of learner-centric education follow:

- Alt School: https://www.altschool.com/ is one where educators and technologists are working together streamlining classroom operations, and developing tools to help create opportunities and environments to improve learning.

- High Tech High Schools focus on project-based learning: https://www.hightechhigh.org/.

- MIT Lab in Massachusetts, which has a reputation known to push the boundaries in learning by doing, hosted a Connected Learning Summit http://connectedlearningsummit.org/ in August 2018.

- Renee Hobbs at the Media Education Lab in Providence Rhode Island is a pioneer in this field, developing media education curricula from Kindergarten up and running leadership forums in understanding digital literacy.

- In Australia, Methodist Ladies College (MLC) is the first school worldwide to embed pioneering virtual reality technology *ImmerseMe* into its language curriculum. The program uses voice recognition software and puts students in an immersive environment where they can practice a language with a native speaker. The technology is now the backbone of the school's language program.

- At Xavier College in Melbourne, coding robots and building motorized rovers have been part of the curriculum for Middle and Senior Years for some time.

- At Melbourne Girl's Grammar School (MGGS) students can qualify with a drone pilot certificate as part of their STEM studies.[53]

- I have watched my grandchildren teach themselves magic tricks, how to do Rubik's cube, how to build a shed, learn a language fluently by chatting with others across the globe, make cement and reinforce a pavement and go online to make sense of tertiary lecturers who don't know how to teach. If they want to know something the smart phone and the internet are the first stop.

Such initiatives should not be fringe activities; technology needs to become a central component of the education curriculum now the information revolution has transformed every aspect of society.

4. Preparation for the workplace. What are the skills needed?

Children actively changing their media usage and consequent self-learning behaviours are developing skills that will hold them in good stead across their longer life span, yet many schools in the system are still failing to adapt. A survey of 1,000 parents by Real Insurance titled Future of Education showed 80% either had no confidence or marginal confidence in the school curriculum and many are worried about how the education system aligns with the needs of future workplaces.[54] The tertiary sector too is lagging behind the needs of employers who are realizing they need to recruit employees who are not simply knowledge specialists but people who are adaptable and willing to keep learning as technology transforms the workplace.

Linda Darling-Hammond, (2018) President and CEO of the Learning Policy Institute and the Charles E. Ducommun Emeritus Professor of Education at the Stanford Graduate School of Education, describes teaching 'as the profession on which all other professions depend'. She argues that memorising information for tests in content silos will no longer prepare kids for the future. They are going to have to work with knowledge that hasn't been discovered yet and technologies that haven't been invented yet, to solve big problems that we haven't been able to solve. They need work in schools that allows them to take up a problem, figure out how to find the resources that will be needed to solve that problem, work with others to design a solution, test it, evaluate it, revise it, and be able to generate their own progress in learning. 'That's a very different kind of teaching. [Importantly] It doesn't mean the facts disappear. It doesn't mean that teaching a structured curriculum disappears. But it does mean that the way you approach the curriculum has to be much more focused around that kind of inquiry than simply reading a chapter and answering the questions at the end of the book'.[55]

Teachers need to understand how people learn, and how they learn differently. They need to know how people develop in social, emotional, academic, moral and physical ways. They need to understand the relationship between emotion and learning. You only really learn when you are excited or interested. If you like your teachers you are more likely to learn. Research concludes in Australia that 46% of students are disengaged.[56] If you're fearful or think somebody is going to criticize, you're going to learn less. Teachers also need to know how to build a curriculum that gets kids from wherever they are to the goals set for them.

One successful example of school-to-workplace transition is a program which began in Brooklyn sponsored by IBM in 2011. *Pathways in Technology Early College High Schools* or P-TECH had spread to 100 schools in the US by 2018, and is in pilot programs in Australia. P-TECH schools are innovative public schools (called State Schools in Australia) spanning grades 9 to 14. In the model, local employers partner with schools, TAFEs/RTOs and Universities to strengthen students' prospects of a successful transition to work by ensuring they develop the technical and personal skills employers are looking for.[57]

In the US, within six years, students graduate with a no-cost associate degree in applied science, engineering, computers or other competitive STEM disciplines, along with the skills and knowledge they need to continue their studies or step more easily into high-growth, 'new collar' jobs. These are positions in some of the nation's fastest-growing industries.

In January 2017, Hunter River High School in New South Wales introduced an innovative P-TECH-styled skills-based program that focuses on aeronautical and related aerospace industries, and provides an industry-supported pathway for students to achieve a post-school qualification in an area of growing local employment demand. The school has worked in collaboration with other education and training providers and a number of major locally-based employer partners including BAE Systems Australia, Jetstar, Varley Group Engineering and Amp control. All Year 10 students at the school commenced a P-TECH immersion program in 2017, and took part in a range of industry-supported learning experiences to extend their education beyond the classroom and help them to better understand the relevance of their learning and how it can be applied in the workplace.

In the workplaces of the future it's not just STEM skills that will be needed. If AI means robots will take over many of today's jobs, social skills will be needed for many positions in the service industries. P-TECH is a model that could be applied to the service sector as well. Social media communication skills can also be fostered through imaginative uses of new technologies.

What this all adds up to is the need to integrate education and communication policies for children. Entertainment media should not be regulated independently from the education sector. We need a whole-of-Government approach towards the entertainment we regulate and subsidise for young people and the schooling they receive.

Conclusion

Kids now inhabit a world that could not have been imagined even two decades ago and there is no going back. They are a new breed bearing little resemblance to those who were seen but not heard, who sat passively accepting school routines, viewed what was put in front of them and were exposed to life's experiences as adults thought fit. Now there is no clear, controlled transition from primary schooler, to tween, to teen. Social media has brought young people together and opened their eyes, given opportunities, independence, freedom to explore, information and knowledge beyond the experience of earlier generations. Despite the luddites, the PC brigade and the professional doomsayers, most kids are more resilient than we used to think when we adults pulled all the strings. Now they are a tough audience to capture. They have so many options. They like and seek a challenge; they love to engage, compete and share; they want to laugh, and they have advice for us about their needs and interests. They must be involved in the decisions affecting their education and entertainment that comes to them through new media, if projects are to succeed. We need project producers to respond to today's kids' interests with new ideas and take on the challenge they represent. We need schools and teachers who can nurture children's voracious appetites for learning with direction fit for purpose for this century.

In this essay I have described some examples from around the world of producers coming to grips with new technology and new ways of storytelling. Australia, once a leader in programming for children, no longer punches above its weight as we once did and Finland now does: innovation is far too rare.

As the Government is currently pondering new regulations to support relevant children's Australian media content, there's a chance to rectify this deficit. Government subsidy of children's media entertainment programs is justified culturally but should also aim to facilitate their education, mastery and understanding of media. Regulations should not be just about sanitizing and controlling content; they must aim to support children's capacities to negotiate the cyber-world and to stimulate their learning and creativity. Additionally, more clarity is required for teachers from school and curriculum authorities regarding media literacy instruction and the priority it should be given in Australian classrooms.[58] Such an approach requires a radical re-think of our children's regulatory system and their education curriculum.

We must move on from the 40-year-old quotas on commercial broadcasters to a comprehensive media development innovation program, which could include relief from quotas in the commercial sector for an annual payment to an innovation fund of $10 million from each network in the first year; a more focused innovative programming role for the public broadcasters ABC and SBS in service to children and young people; and a new approach to media literacy curricula in schools supporting learner-centric projects that develop initiative and adaptability as skills to enable students to transition to the rapidly changing workplaces of the future.

Australia could thus develop a new agency dedicated to the support of wide-ranging innovative media projects for children's entertainment and education. These projects might include games, multi-platform narratives, collaborative projects or children's own productions which should have an educational and innovative purpose, as well as being entertaining. Media literacy education should be extended through the education system to exploit the learning potential of all forms of digital media and their social impact for the future of children. There should be a concerted research effort to document the links between children's media use and their learning in order to initiate effective educational and entertaining projects for children. Within an integrated education/communication policy, we need projects that inspire.

Bob Dylan's poetic words of advice, *The Times They Are A-Changin'*, sung to writers and critics, congressmen and senators, mothers and fathers to 'please heed the call' was written in 1964. They are apposite 55 years later.

The Australian and Children's Screen Content Review (announced 6 May 2017 by the Minister for Communications, Mitch Fifield), awaits a response. My submission – *What really happened to Australian Children's Television? And Where to from here?* – was written in July 2017.[59]

Notes

1. Betsy Morris (2018), 'The new tech avengers of Silicon Valley', *Australian*, 7 July; Nicholas Confessore (2018), 'Unlikely activists take on Silicon Valley – and win', *Australian*, 20 August (reprinted from the *New York Times*).

2. Friend, Tad (2018), 'Superior Intelligence: Do the perils of AI exceed its promise?', *New Yorker*, 14 May.

3. ACMA (2007), *Media and Communications in Australian Families*, Australian Communications and Media Authority, Melbourne.

4. Laurie. Victoria (2018), 'Parents 'not ready' for digital oversight', *Australian*, 9 July.

5. Edgar, Patricia (1977a), *Children & Screen Violence*, University of Queensland Press.

6. Houston, Melinda (2008), 'Television Preview', *The Age*, 9 November.

7. Dow, Aisha (2018), 'Poor body image starts to develop as young as eight', *The Age*, 15 August.

8. https://variety.com/2018/tv/news/insatiable-fat-shaming-netflix-show1202882565/#utm_medium=social&utm_source=email&utm_campaign=social_bar&utm_content=bottom&utm_id=1202882565.

9. Cooney Carillo, Jenny (2018), 'Sweet revenge', *The Age, Sunday Life*, 19 August.

10. Urban, Rebecca (2018), 'Phones call the shots for our young', *Australian,* 2 August.

11. Hyndman, Brendon & Noella Mackenzie (2018), 'Eight Things that should be included in Screen guidelines for Children, *Conversation*, 24 April; Holzer, Sophie & Damien Maher (2018), 'We asked five experts: should mobile phones be banned?', *Conversation*, 28 June.

12. Burke, Justin (2018), 'Non-work ranting on social media can kill a career', *Australian*, 31 May.

13. Hersh, Seymour (2018), *Reporter: A Memoir*, Allen Lane.

14. *New York Times* (2018), 'Social media screening for millions of visitors to US', reprinted in *The Age,* 1 April.

15. Menand, Louis (2018), 'Nowhere to hide: Why do we care about privacy?', *New Yorker,* 18 June.

16. Biggs, Tim (2018), 'Games buyers go old school', *The Age,* 25 August.

17. Clark, Gabriel (2018), 'Ten of Australia's best literary comics', *Conversation,* 11 September.

18. Edgar, Patricia (2006), *Bloodbath: A memoir of Australian Television,* MUP.

19. Australian Broadcasting Control Board (1976), *Report of the Advisory Committee on Program Standards,* February, Melbourne.

20. Vaidhyanathan, Siva (2018), *Anti-Social Media, How Facebook Disconnects us and Undermines Democracy*, Oxford University Press.

21. Sweney, Mark (2018), 'Younger viewers now watch Netflix more than the BBC, says corporation, *Guardian*, 28 March.

22. Dickson, Jeremy (2018), 'BBC releases sharing app for under-13s', http://www.bbc.co.uk/mediacentre/latestnews/2018/cbbc-buzz, 6 April.

23. Ofcom (2018), *Children's content review – update: Assessing the current provision of children's programs on TV and online,*

https://www.ofcom.org.uk/consultations-and-statements/
category-2/childrens-content-review, published 24 July.

24. Flint, Joe (2018), 'Nickelodeon dumps top producer as
    changing tastes spark ratings slide', *Australian,* 6 April.

25. Buckland, Jenny (2018), '7 Things Australia Can Learn
    from the Ofcom report into Children's Content', 20 August,
    https://blog-actf.com.au/7-things-australia-can-learn-from-
    the-ofcom-report/.

26. Buckland, Jenny (2018), '2018 shaping up to be a critical
    year for Australian children's television', http://blog-actf.
    com.au, 31 January.

27. Max, D.T. (2018), 'Posts modern: An innovative teen drama
    advances, minute by minute, on your social-media feed',
    New Yorker, 18 June 18.

28. Quibell-Young, Nikos (2018), 'Chill over your kids playing
    Fortnite', *Australian,* 26 July; Swan, David (2018), 'Hooked,
    online and sinking deep into Fortnite', *Australian,* 1 July;
    Swan, David (2018), 'New game in town', *Australian,* 31
    May; King, Madonna (2018), 'Game that's making teen
    boys brawl and bawl', *The Age,* 8 June; Paumgarten, Nick
    (2018), 'Weaponized; How Fortnite has created a mass social
    gathering', *New Yorker,* 21 May.

29. Child, Ben (2018), 'Brie Larsen's Captain Marvel reshapes
    the future for superheroes', *Guardian*, 13 September.

30. Stuart, Keith (2018), 'Who is Captain Marvel? Forty
    years after her debut, a female superhero takes flight',
    Guardian, 30 July; Cooney, Jenny (2018), 'Marvel's
    original superheroine embraces feminine side', *The Age,*
    6 July; Metcalf, Stephen (2018), 'Clobbering time: How
    superheroes killed the movie star', *New Yorker,* 28 May;
    Mathieson, Craig (2018), 'The fantastical art of being
    someone else', *Sunday Age,* 3 June; Sun, Michael (2018),
    'The rise of the female superhero', *The Age,* 12 January;
    Needleman, Sarah E. (2018), 'Knowing how to shoot 'em
    ain't enough …', *Australian,* 2 August.

31. Justin Burke (2018), 'Back to the Drawing Board', *Australian Review,* 11–12 August.

32. Gary Nunn (2018), 'Outrage at Disney casting Jack Whitehall to play a gay character is misguided', *Guardian*, 15 August.

33. 'Ruby Rose cast as lesbian superhero Batwoman in new TV series', *Guardian,* 8 August 2018, http://www.theguardian. com/culture/2018/aug/08/ruby-rose-cast-as-lesbian-superhero-batwoman-in-new-tv-series?CMP=share_btn_link.

34. Quinn, Karl (2018), 'Thriller for the digital age', *The Age* EG, 14 September.

35. Moncrieff, Sean (2017), 'Is Peppa Pig a fat-shaming Feminazi?', *Irish Times Magazine,* 9 December.

36. Aisbett, Kate (2000), *20 Years of C: Children's television programs and regulation 1979–1999*, ABA, ACTF and AFFC, Sydney.

37. Carmody, Brode (2018), 'Netflix failed to warn of 'strong suicide themes', *The Age,* 15 August.

38. Edgar, Patricia (1977b), 'The Media as a Rival Seat of Learning', Tenth Anniversary Meredith Memorial Lecture, in *The Role of Universities Today,* La Trobe University, pp. 45–62.

39. Gardner, Howard (1983), *Frames of Mind: The theory of Multiple Intelligences*, Basic Books, New York.

40. Edgar, *Bloodbath.*

41. Lehmann, Claire (2018), 'Hard to discern whether it's coddling, ideology or both causing campus riots', *Weekend Australian,* 8–9 September; Glancy, Josh (2018), 'The Rise of the Snowflake Generation', *Weekend Australian*, 8–9 September.

42. Lehmann, Megan (2018), 'Just Go KYS xo', *Weekend Australian.*

43. Benoit, David (2018), 'Activists demand Apple lift its game', *Australian*, 9 January.

44. Morris, 'The new tech avengers of Silicon Valley'; Confessore, 'Unlikely activists take on Silicon Valley – and win'.

45. Taylor, Charlie (2017), 'Angry Birds Team in its element with Big Bang Theory', *Irish Times*, 14 December.

46. http://www.q2l.org/.

47. Vaidhyanathan, *Anti-Social Media*.

48. Edgar, 'The Media as a Rival Seat of Learning'.

49. Ofcom, *Children's content review – update*, p. 29.

50. *Guardian,* 28 March 2018.

51. Simpson, John (2018), 'Social media has armed the young', *Australian,* 18 April.

52. Kakutani, Michiko (2018), *The Death of Truth*, William Collins, p. 77.

53. 'Innovation in education', *Sunday Age,* special supplement, 12 August 2018.

54. Pallavi, Singhai (2018), 'Parents not convinced by curriculum', *The Age,* 23 July.

55. http://ed.stanford.edu/news/teaching-profession-which-all-other-professions-depend-linda-darling-hammond-transforming.

56. Owen, Jan (2018), *Australian, Deal*, No. 106, August.

57. Fister Gale (2018), 'P-Tech a lesson in closing high-tech skills gap', http://www.workforce.com, 16 May.

58. Nettlefold, Jocelyn, and Williams, Kathleen (2018), *Insight Five: A snapshot of Media Literacy in Australian Schools,* Institute for the Study of Social Change, University of Tasmania. utas.edu.au/social-change.

59. Edgar, Patricia (2017), *What really happened to Australian Children's Television? And Where to from here?,* Submission to the Australian and Children's Screen Content Review, July 2017, www.patriciaedgaranddonedgar.com.

About the Author

Dr Patricia Edgar AM, BA, B.Ed (Hons) (Melbourne University), MA (Stanford University), PhD (La Trobe University), Hon. D.Litt (University of WA), Doctor of Letters (La Trobe University).

Patricia Edgar was Chair of the Australian Broadcasting Control Board's Advisory Committee on Program Standards (1975–76) and a Member of the Australian Broadcasting Control Board (1975–76). In those roles she was the architect of the C classification for children's television. She was Chair of the Australian Broadcasting Tribunal's Children's Program Committee 1978–84 and oversaw the implementation of the Children's Television Standards (CTS) and the Drama Quota. She was the founding director of the Australian Children's Television Foundation (ACTF) 1982–2002. In that role she produced over 174 hours of television drama which won more than 100 national and international awards and sold into more than 100 countries. She was Deputy Chair of the Film Finance Corporation 1988–1996, Founder of the World Summit Movement (1995) and was Chair of the World Summit on Media for Children Foundation (1999–2017). Currently she is Deputy Chair of the Foundation.

www.patriciaedgaranddonedgar.com

9 781925 801514